ANIMAL BABIES

A TRUE BOOK

by

Ann O. Squire

Children's Press®
A Division of Scholastic Inc.

New York Toronto London Auckland Sydney
Mexico City New Delhi Hong Kong
Danbury, Connecticut

A horse colt and its mother

Content Consultant
Kathy Carlstead, Ph.D.
Honolulu Zoo

Reading Consultant
Nanci R. Vargus, Ed.D.
Primary Multiage Teacher
Decatur Township Schools,
Indianapolis, IN

Dedication
To Evan

The photograph on the cover shows adult and baby emperor penguins. The photograph on the title page shows adult and baby dwarf rabbits.

Library of Congress Cataloging-in-Publication Data

Squire, Ann.
    Animal babies / by Ann O. Squire.
        p. cm. — (A True book)
    Includes bibliographical references and index (p.).
    ISBN 0-516-22188-4   0-516-25995-4 (pbk.)
    1. Animals—Infancy—Juvenile literature. [1. Animals—Infancy.] I. Title.
II. Series.

QL763 .S72 2001
591.3'9—dc21   00-057024

GROLIER
PUBLISHING

©2001 Children's Press®
A Division of Scholastic Inc.
All rights reserved. Published simultaneously in Canada.
Printed in the United States of America.
1 2 3 4 5 6 7 8 9 10 R 10 09 08 07 06 05 04 03 02 01

Contents

Giraffe calves look like tiny versions of their parents (top). A caterpillar (bottom left) looks very different from the adult butterfly it becomes (bottom right).

Everyone Starts Out as a Baby

Some animal babies are tiny versions of adults. Others look so different from their parents that you'd never know the babies and adults were related.

Baby animals start life in different ways. Some hatch

Mammals, such as koalas (above), are cared for by their parents. Insects, such as praying mantises (right), are on their own from the moment they are born.

out of eggs and some are born live. Some are cared for by their parents and some are on their own from the beginning.

Out of the Egg

All animals must grow and develop before joining the outside world. Birds, amphibians, fish, and many reptiles do this inside an egg.

When we think of eggs, we usually think of birds' eggs. A baby bird enters the world by hatching out of a

Wild turkey chicks hatching from their eggs

hard-shelled egg laid by its mother.

Many birds incubate their eggs by sitting on them to keep them warm until they hatch. Emperor and king penguins, which live in Antarctica, warm their eggs by resting them on top of their feet!

A king penguin incubating an egg

Many snakes begin life in eggs too, but snake eggs are tough and leathery rather than hard and brittle. A snake called the Indian rock python lays between 50 and 100 eggs at a time. Then she coils her huge body around the eggs to warm and protect them. Since snakes are cold blooded, the mother rock python has to twitch her muscles to create heat.

During the two months it takes for the eggs to hatch, the

A mother python curled around her eggs

mother python stays in one place and does not even eat. Imagine how hungry she is by the time her babies arrive!

Frogs lay their jellylike eggs in water.

Frogs lay their eggs in jellylike clumps along the edge of a pond. Mother frogs do not take care of their eggs. As soon as the eggs are laid, the parents leave.

When a baby frog, or tadpole, hatches, it doesn't look anything like an adult frog. It has a tail, it has no legs or eyes, and it is

Newly hatched tadpoles have tails and no legs.

completely helpless. Soon, it grows eyes and teeth and starts to swim around, eating almost anything it can find.

During the next few months, an amazing change takes place. The tadpole grows legs, its tail begins to shrink, and it looks more and more like its parents. Finally, the tiny, fishlike tadpole is transformed into a grown-up frog.

As a tadpole grows up, it sprouts legs and its tail shrinks.

Born Live

Some baby animals do not hatch from eggs. Instead, they develop inside their mother's body until they are ready to be born. These animals are called mammals.

Mammals differ from other kinds of animals in

Polar bears are mammals.

other ways as well. They are warm blooded, they usually have hair or fur, and their

All baby mammals, including wild boars, are fed with mother's milk.

babies are fed with milk that comes from the mother.

Some mammals, such as humans, elephants, and whales, usually give birth to only one baby at a time. These babies spend a long time growing inside the mother before they are born—9 months for humans, a little more than 1 year for whales, and nearly 2 years for elephants.

Large mammals, such as elephants and whales, usually have only one baby at a time.

A litter of kittens

Other mammals, including dogs and cats, have several babies at one time. Before being born, each puppy or kitten grows in its own water-filled sac inside the mother's body. A group of puppies or kittens born at the same time is called a litter.

Kangaroo babies are less than 1 inch (2.5 centimeters) long when they are born.

A newborn joey inside its mother's pouch (below) and a mother kangaroo with an older joey in her pouch (left)

These tiny creatures are much too small to live outside their mother's body. So just after birth, the newborn kangaroo, called a joey, crawls up its mother's fur and into a pouch on her belly. It stays there until it is big enough to live on its own. Kangaroos and other mammals with pouches are known as marsupials.

Although they are not mammals, sea horse babies also grow in a parent's pouch. But in this case, the parent with the pouch is the father!

The mother sea horse places her eggs in the male's pouch and swims away. She has nothing more to do with

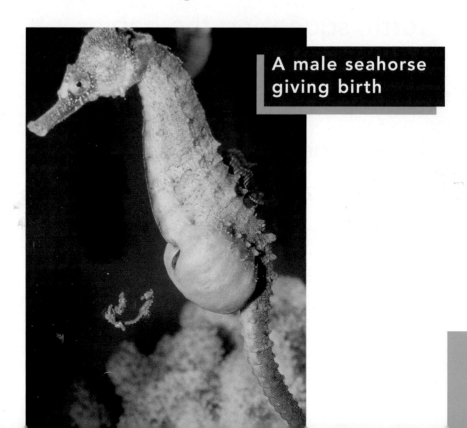

A male seahorse giving birth

her babies. The young sea horses grow inside their father's pouch until they are ready to be born.

When the time is right, the father begins to rock back and forth, squeezing the babies out of the pouch. Although they are only as big as your little fingernail, the baby sea horses do not need any more help from their father. As soon as they leave his pouch, they go off on their own.

An Unusual Mammal

A platypus swimming (above) and a baby platypus (below)

Is it a duck? A beaver? No, it's a duck-billed platypus. This strange creature, with its furry body, ducklike bill, and webbed feet, is actually a mammal. Like all mammals, platypus babies drink their mother's milk. But unlike all other mammals, platypus babies hatch from eggs!

Independent Babies

Some baby animals can see, hear, stand, and walk soon after they are born. Some can even find food for themselves. Newborn babies that need little or no help from their parents are called precocial.

Most precocial animals have lots of enemies and many live

Rhinoceros calves, like other precocial animal babies, can see, hear, stand, and run right after birth.

in places where it is hard for their parents to protect them. If they could not fend for themselves, they would not survive. Precocial animals include most reptiles, amphibians, and fish, as well as some birds and mammals.

When a baby zebra is born on the African plains, for example, it enters a world filled with lions, cheetahs, hyenas, and other predators. If the newborn cannot keep up with the herd, it will soon become someone's dinner.

Fortunately, a baby zebra can stand and run within an hour after birth. But it still needs to drink its mother's milk and stay close to her for protection.

A newborn zebra colt with its mother (left) and a pair of Canada geese with their goslings (below)

Geese and ducks can walk, swim, and look for their own food soon after they hatch. But like zebras, they need their mother's protection for a while.

A female sea turtle
laying eggs

Some animals, like sea
turtles, never even meet their
parents. At nesting time, the
mother turtle comes up onto
the beach. She digs a hole in
the sand and lays her eggs in it.

After covering the eggs fully, she heads back out sea, never to return.

The buried eggs are kept warm by the sun and moist by the damp sand. After two to three months, the eggs hatch and the baby turtles dig their way out. The first thing they do is make a mad dash for the water. It's lucky that they know how to walk as soon as they hatch, beacuse that trip across the beach is dangerous!

Sea-turtle hatchlings digging their way out of the sand and heading for the ocean

Seabirds and other animals are just waiting to pounce on the tiny turtles.

Once they reach the sea, the turtles know how to swim and find their own food, even though they've never learned how from their parents!

Helpless Babies

Unlike the sea turtle, many animals are completely helpless at birth. Animal babies that depend on their parents for food, warmth, and protection are called altricial. The babies of most mammals and birds need lots of care and protection after birth.

Altricial animal babies, such as puppies, need lots of care from their parents.

Have you ever seen a litter of newborn puppies? They cannot walk, see, or hear. They can smell, however, and this helps them find one of their mother's nipples so that they can begin getting her milk.

Most birds other than ducks and geese need a lot of help from their parents when they are young. Baby robins are born without feathers, so they cannot fly out of the nest to look for food. This keeps the parent

Hungry robin chicks

birds very busy searching for worms and insects to bring back to their hungry chicks.

Baby penguins are born with tiny, soft feathers called down. Down is not waterproof, so the penguin chicks cannot go into the sea to catch fish for themselves. The parents take turns bringing food for their hungry babies and sitting on the nest.

As the chicks grow, they need more and more food. This means that both parents have

Adult emperor penguins guarding a group of penguin chicks

to work full-time to find food. While the parents are gone, they leave the chicks in groups guarded by a few adults—sort of like day care for penguins!

Animal Families

For people, families are very important. Your family keeps you safe from harm and teaches you the things you need to know as you are growing up.

Many animal families do the same things for their young. When a baby elephant is born, it joins a family that includes

A family of northern fur seals

A family of African elephants

its mother, aunts, cousins, sisters and brothers. The baby elephant stays close to its mother, but all the adults in the group help to protect the baby. They teach it how to avoid danger and where to find food.

If the baby is a male, he leaves the family when he is about ten years old. But a female elephant lives with her mother and her other female relatives all her life.

Most animals don't spend that long with their families. But in the time they are together, the adults teach the young everything they need to know in order to survive on their own.

Tiger cubs are small and helpless when they are born. They depend on their mother for everything. But they grow quickly, and when they are two months old, they are ready to follow the mother as she hunts. They learn what it takes to be a successful hunter by watching her. They also practice their hunting skills by chasing and pouncing on their brothers and sisters.

By the time the cubs are
2 1/2 years old, they have
learned all they can from their
mother. Now it is time for
them to go out on their own.

To Find Out More

Here are some additional resources to help you learn more about animal babies:

Books

Collard, Sneed B. **Making Animal Babies.** Houghton Mifflin Company, 2000.

Craig, Claire. **Animal Babies.** Time Life, 1996.

Maynard, Christopher. **Amazing Animal Babies.** Eyewitness Juniors, no. 25, 1993.

Stuart, Gene S. **Animal Families.** National Geographic Society, 1997.

Organizations and Online Sites

Animal Planet

www.Animal.Discovery.com

Information on all kinds of animals, as well as links to nature shows on the Discovery Channel.

Baby Pictures

http://www.squirrel-rehab. org/pictures/index.html

See lots of pictures of animal babies.

Names of Animals, Babies, and Groups of Animals

http://www.Enchanted Learning.com/subjects/ animals/Animalbabies.html

Did you know that a baby swan is called a cygnet, a baby llama is called a cria, and a baby fish is called a fry? Find out about these and lots of other names for baby animals.

National Geographic

www.nationalgeographic. com

A wealth of interesting information on animals and nature.

Important Words

altricial animal that depends on its parents
for protection, food, and care when it is
a baby

cold blooded having a body temperature
that changes with the environment

down covering of soft, fluffy feathers

generate to create

incubate to keep something warm

marsupial mammal that carries its young in
a pouch in the mother's abdomen

precocial animal that can move about, find
food, and get along on its own when it is
first born

predator animal that captures and eats
other animals

siblings brothers or sisters

warm blooded maintaining a nearly con-
stant body temperature

Index

Meet the Author

Ann O. Squire has a Ph.D. in animal behavior. Before becoming a writer, she studied African electric fish, rats, and other animals. Dr. Squire has written several books on animals and their behavior, including *Anteaters, Sloths, and Armadillos* and *Spiders of North America*. She lives with her children, Emma and Evan, in Bedford, New York.